NEW EDITION

GRAMMAR STEP BY STEP

with Pictures

Ralph Boggs • Robert Dixson

Longman

Grammar Step by Step with Pictures

Pearson Education, 10 Bank Street, White Plains, NY 10606

Senior acquisitions editor: Virginia Blanford
Development editor: Katherine Rawson
Associate managing editor: Sandra Pike
Marketing manager: Joseph Chapple
Senior manufacturing buyer: Ray Keating
Cover design: Patricia Wosczyk
Text design: Patricia Wosczyk
Text composition: TSI Graphics
Text font: Frutiger, 11pt
Text art: Luis Briseño

LONGMAN ON THE **WEB**

Longman.com offers online resources for teachers and students. Access our Companion Websites, our online catalog, and our local offices around the world.

Visit us at **longman.com**.

ISBN: 0-13-1411756

Printed in the United States of America
26   17

PREFACE

Grammar Step by Step with Pictures was first published in 1956 under the title *English Step by Step,* and was one of the first texts for English language learners available. Any text that remains not only popular but useful over four decades clearly offers an extremely effective methodology to the teacher and student. The popularity of *Grammar Step by Step* stems from the ease with which the instructor can pass on essential grammar and vocabulary to the learner, or the learner can work independently through the progression of lessons to review and practice grammar already studied.

In the decade since the last edition, American culture has seen many changes. Technology, gender roles, and diversity are reflected in the updated illustrations of the new edition. Also, the lessons have been re-ordered slightly to reflect the current standard syllabi of beginning to intermediate courses, so the book can be used as a supplement or a perfect partner to any standard English language course for young adults or adults.

This new edition of *Grammar Step by Step with Pictures* contains 46 lessons that constitute a series of simple, graduated steps designed to give the student a maximum sense of accomplishment. Each lesson consists of two pages of presentation followed by four pages of focused practice. Along with the essential structures of English, over 800 vocabulary words are presented and then recycled throughout the text to reinforce learning.

This edition of *Grammar Step by Step* also includes a Quick Grammar Reference section, a handy resource to which students can turn for quick review of essential principles.

CONTENTS

1 Questions and Answers...2

2 Negative Statements...6

3 Subject Pronouns; Simple Present Tense: *To Be—Affirmative*...10

4 Simple Present Tense: *To Be—Negative*...16

5 Simple Present Tense: *To Be—Questions*...22

6 Questions with *Where*; Prepositions...28

7 *There is, There are; Some, Any*...34

8 Possessive Adjectives; Possessive Pronouns...40

9 The Indefinite Article: *A or An*...46

10 Plural of Nouns...52

11 Demonstrative Pronouns: *Singular and Plural*...58

12 Numbers: *Cardinals and Ordinals*...64

13 Telling Time; Counting Money...68

14 Descriptive Adjectives...74

15 Possessive Nouns...78

16 REVIEW...82

17 Simple Present Tense: *Affirmative*...84

18 Simple Present Tense: *Negative*...90

19 Simple Present Tense: *Questions*...96

20 *Yes/No* Questions and Short Answers;

Information Questions...100

21 Present Continuous Tense: *Affirmative*...104

22 Present Continuous Tense: *Negative*...110

23 Present Continuous Tense: *Questions*...114

24   **Object Pronouns...118**

25   **Past Tense: *To Be—Affirmative*...122**

26   **Past Tense: *To Be—Negative and Questions*...128**

27   **Past Tense: *Regular Verbs—Affirmative*...134**

28   **Past Tense: *Irregular Verbs—Affirmative*...140**

29   **Past Tense: *Regular and Irregular Verbs—Negative*...146**

30   **Past Tense: *Regular and Irregular Verbs—Questions*...150**

31   **REVIEW...154**

32   **Future Tense with *Going to*: *Affirmative*...156**

33   **Future Tense with *Going to*: *Negative and Questions*...160**

34   **Adjectives and Adverbs...164**

35   **Adjectives and Adverbs: *Comparative Forms*...168**

36   **Adjectives and Adverbs: *Superlative Forms*...174**

37   **Future Tense with *Will*: *Affirmative*...178**

38   **Future Tense with *Will*: *Negative and Questions*...182**

39   **Reflexive and Intensive Pronouns...186**

40   **Imperative...192**

41   **Present Perfect Tense: *Affirmative*...196**

42   **Present Perfect Tense: *Negative*...200**

43   **Present Perfect Tense: *Questions*...204**

44   **The Calendar, Seasons, and Weather...208**

45   **House and Furniture...212**

46   **REVIEW...216**

      Quick Grammar Reference...220

      Vocabulary...235

QUESTIONS AND ANSWERS

1

What's this?*
It's a pen.**

2

What's this?
It's a pencil.

3

What's this?
It's a computer.

4

What's this?
It's a radio.

5

What's this?
It's a table.

6

What's this?
It's a chair.

7

What's this?
It's a shirt.

8

What's this?
It's a suit.

*What's is the contraction of what is.
**It's is the contraction of it is.

9

What's this?
It's a dress.

10

What's this?
It's a skirt.

11

What's this?
It's a sock.

12

What's this?
It's a shoe.

13

What's this?
It's a dog.

14

What's this?
It's a cat.

15

What's this?
It's a tree.

16

What's this?
It's a flower.

Practice

Answer the questions in complete sentences.

1. What's this?
It's a cat.

2. What's this?
It's a tree.

3. What's this?

4. What's this?

5. What's this?

6. What's this?

7. What's this?

8. What's this?

VOCABULARY	a	chair	dog	flower	it	pen
	cat	computer	dress	is	it's	pencil

9. What's this?

10. What's this?

11. What's this?

12. What's this?

13. What's this?

14. What's this?

15. What's this?

16. What's this?

radio	shoe	sock	table	tree	what	what's
shirt	skirt	suit	this			

2 NEGATIVE STATEMENTS

This isn't a sock.*
It's a shoe.

This isn't a radio.
It's a newspaper.

This isn't a table.
It's a desk.

This isn't a shirt.
It's a coat.

This isn't a shoe.
It's a boot.

This isn't a shirt.
It's a skirt.

This isn't a pair of boots.
It's a pair of pants.

This isn't a pair of shoes.
It's a pair of socks.

*Isn't is the contraction of is not.

This isn't a computer.
It's a TV.

This isn't a desk.
It's a chair.

This isn't a pencil.
It's a pen.

This isn't a chair.
It's a table.

This isn't a school.
It's a house.

This isn't a house.
It's a school.

This isn't a cat.
It's a dog.

This isn't a flower.
It's a tree.

Practice

Answer the questions in complete sentences. First give a negative answer, and then give an affirmative answer.

1. Is this a pen?
No, it isn't a pen.*
It's a pencil.

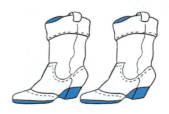

2. Is this a dress?
No, it isn't a dress.
It's a coat.

3. Is this a skirt?

4. Is this a pair of pants?

5. Is this a radio?

6. Is this a shoe?

7. Is this a shirt?

8. Is this a chair?

| VOCABULARY | boot | coat | desk | house | isn't | newspaper |

**It isn't* or *it's not* may be used.

9. Is this a dog?

10. Is this a table?

11. Is this a school?

12. Is this a house?

13. Is this a tree?

14. Is this a computer?

15. Is this a suit?

16. Is this a pencil?

no	not	pair	pants	school	TV

SUBJECT PRONOUNS; SIMPLE PRESENT TENSE: *To Be—Affirmative*

SUBJECT PRONOUNS

	Singular	Plural
1st person	I	we
2nd person	you	you
3rd person	he she it	they

It refers to a thing or an animal, but never a person.*
They refers to things, animals, or people.

TO BE

	FULL FORMS		CONTRACTED FORMS	
	Singular	Plural	Singular	Plural
1st person	I am	we are	I'm	we're
2nd person	you are	you are	you're	you're
3rd person	he she } is it	they are	he's she's it's	they're

When used with subject pronouns, the verb forms are usually shortened.

I'm a student.

Jim and I are students.

*He and *she* are usually used with animals that are pets.

3

You're an accountant.

4

You and Ellen are accountants.

5

The man is a mechanic.

6

The women are mechanics.*

7

The woman is a doctor.

8

The men are doctors.*

9

It is a chair.

10

They are chairs.

*The plural forms of *man* and *woman* are irregular: *men, women.*

Practice

A. Fill in the blanks with the correct form of the verb *to be*. Then, say each sentence, using the contracted form wherever possible.

1. I ____am____ a teacher.
I'm a teacher.

2. Jill and I ____are____ doctors.

3. They _____ mechanics.

4. He _____ a doctor.

5. They _____ chairs.

6. Tom and Paula _____ students.

7. It _____ a cat.

8. We _____ teachers.

9. You and Joe _____ accountants.

10. She _____ a mechanic.

11. They _____ flowers.

12. I _____ a student.

B. Substitute the words in this sentence. Use contractions when possible.

EXAMPLE: *I'm a doctor.*   (you (singular) / they)
You're a doctor.
They're doctors.

1. you (plural)

2. they

3. we

4. you (singular)

5. she

6. Joe

7. he

8. Ana

9. Ana and Jack

10. you and Mike

11. Ellen and I

12. Al and Anita

13. Roy

Practice

C. Answer the questions in complete sentences. Use the contracted forms of the verb whenever possible.

1. Are they shoes or boots?

They're boots.

2. Are you a doctor or an accountant?

3. Is it a skirt or a shirt?

4. Are Jean and John students or accountants?

5. Is the person a man or a woman?

6. Is she a doctor or a mechanic?

7. Are they pens or pencils?

8. Are they dogs or cats?

9. Is it a TV or a computer?

SIMPLE PRESENT TENSE: *To Be—Negative*

Form the negative of *to be* by placing *not* after the verb.

NEGATIVE	Singular	Plural
1st person	I am not	we are not
2nd person	you are not	you are not
3rd person	he she it } is not	they are not

Contracted forms are commonly used. There are two contracted forms.

CONTRACTED FORMS	Singular	Plural	Singular	Plural
1st person	I'm not	we're not	I'm not	we aren't
2nd person	you're not	you're not	you aren't	you aren't
3rd person	he's she's it's } not	they're not	he she it } isn't	they aren't

I'm not a lawyer.
I'm a police officer.

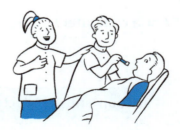

We're not teachers.
We're dentists.

3

You're not a teacher.
You're a student.

 4

You're not doctors.
You're lawyers.

 5

She's not a student.
She's a mechanic.

6

They're not shoes.
They're socks.

 7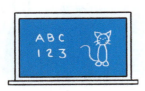

It's not a computer.
It's a chalkboard.

8

They're not horses.
They're elephants.

 9

It's not a radio.
It's a calculator.

10

They're not cats.
They're rabbits.

Practice

A. Substitute the words in this sentence. Use two contracted forms for each substitution when possible.

> EXAMPLE: *I'm* not a lawyer. (he/the men)
> *He's not a lawyer. He isn't a lawyer.*
> *The men aren't lawyers.*

1. you (plural)

2. Susan

3. Bill

4. she

5. the woman

6. the man

7. they

8. we

9. I

10. the women

11. you (singular)

12. Jack and I

13. Ellen and Tom

14. Christine

B. Change the sentences to a contracted form of the negative.

1. Linda's a teacher.
   Linda's not a teacher.   OR
   Linda isn't a teacher.

2. We're police officers.
   We're not police officers.   OR
   We aren't police officers.

3. He's a dentist.

4. It's a rabbit.

5. It's a calculator.

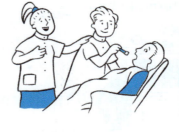

6. She's a doctor.

7. Al's a lawyer.

8. They're shoes.

9. That's a school.

10. It's a table.

11. You're a teacher.

12. I'm a mechanic.

Practice

C. Answer the questions. First give a negative answer and then an affirmative answer. Use contracted forms in both.

1. Are Joe and Helen doctors?
 No, Joe and Helen aren't doctors.
 They're lawyers.

2. Is this a book?
 No, it's not (or it isn't) a book.
 It's a chalkboard.

3. Are you a teacher?

4. Are you a mechanic?

5. Are they rabbits?

6. Is he a police officer?

7. Are you and Lee dentists?

8. Am I a teacher?

9. Is it a rabbit?

10. Are Judy and Marie teachers?

11. Is that a calculator?

12. Are they shoes?

13. Are they boots?

14. Are they tables?

VOCABULARY

| aren't | chalkboard | elephant | lawyer | rabbit |
| calculator | dentist | horse | police officer | |

SIMPLE PRESENT TENSE: *To Be—Questions*

Form questions with *to be* by placing the verb before the subject. Add a question mark at the end of the question.

QUESTIONS	Singular		Plural	
1st person	Am	I?	Are	we?
2nd person	Are	you?	Are	you?
3rd person	Is	he she? it	Are	they?

Am I a teacher?
Yes, you're a teacher.

Are you a movie star?
Yes, I'm a movie star.

Is Ms. Lane a student?
Yes, she's a student.

Is Steve a nurse?
Yes, he's a nurse.

Is Mrs. Riva an artist?
Yes, she's an artist.

Is he a mail carrier?
Yes, he's a mail carrier.

7

Is this a chicken?
Yes, it's a chicken.

8

Are they word processors?
Yes, they're word processors.

 9

Are you dentists?
Yes, we're dentists.

10

Are Laura and Bill police officers?
Yes, they're police officers.

 11

Are they musicians?
Yes, they're musicians.

12

Are Barbara and Joy doctors?
Yes, they're doctors.

 13

Are they good dancers?
Yes, they're good dancers.

14

Are these bananas?
Yes, they're bananas.

Practice

A. Substitute the subject in this question.

EXAMPLE: Am *I* a dancer?   (Don and Peggy)
Are Don and Peggy dancers?

1. you (plural)

2. you and I

3. we

4. Mrs. Thomas

5. he

6. George and Joe

7. they

8. you (singular)

9. Barbara

10. she

11. Betty and I

12. the man

B. Change the sentences to questions.

1. Mr. Ross is a word processor.
   Is Mr. Ross a word processor?

2. We're musicians.
   Are we musicians?

3. You're a computer programmer.

4. They're artists.

5. It is a rabbit.

6. The man is a nurse.

7. The woman is a police officer.

8. It is a banana.

9. He's a waiter.

10. He is a mail carrier.

11. Sarah is a movie star.

12. It is a chicken.

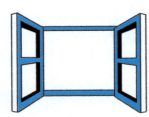

13. It is a window.

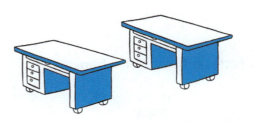

14. They are desks.

Practice

C. Answer the questions in complete sentences.

1. Are you an artist or a dancer?

2. Is Miss Pace a musician or a dentist?

3. Are they chickens or rabbits?

4. Are Dr. James and I doctors or dentists?

5. Is this a flower or a banana?

VOCABULARY	artist	chicken	Dr.
	banana	computer programmer	DVD player
	bird	dancer	fish

6. Is it a fish or a bird?

7. Are they word processors or mail carriers?

8. Is this a DVD player or a computer?

9. Are they pens or pencils?

10. Are they elephants or horses?

mail courier	Mr.	musician	window
Miss	Mrs.	nurse	word processor
movie star	Ms.	waiter	

6 QUESTIONS WITH *WHERE*; PREPOSITIONS

Where is a question word. It asks about location. The contraction of *where is* is *where's*. **Where are** is not contracted.

Where is the computer? OR *Where's the computer?*
Where are the computers?

The answer to a *where* question often includes a prepositional phrase that indicates place.

The computer is on the desk.

Where's the lamp?
It's on the desk.

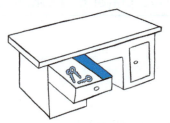

Where are the keys?
They're in the drawer.

Where's the cat?
It's under the sofa.

Where's the suitcase?
It's above the seat.

Where's the little girl?
She's at school.

Where's the big boy?
He's at home.

Where are the boys?
They're in the park.

Where are the bananas?
They're in the bowl.

Where's Walt?
He's behind Susan.

Where's Susan?
She's in front of Walt.

Where's the TV?
It's between the lamp and the chair.

Where are the flowers?
They're between the books and
the lamp.

Practice

A. Fill in the blanks with the correct preposition.

1. The picture is ___*on*___ the wall.

2. The computer is _____ the desk.

3. The girls are _____ home.

4. Mary is _____ Bill.

5. The dog is _____ the chair.

6. The picture is _____ the chair.

7. The TV is _____ the sofa.

8. The cat is _____ the boy and the girl.

B. Here are some answers. Write a *where* question for each one.

1. The keys are on the book.
Where are the keys?

2. The cat is in the suitcase.
Where's the cat?

3. The trees are in the park.

4. Alice is in front of the house.

5. The picture is between the door and the TV.

6. The children are at school.*

7. He's behind the sofa.

8. The mechanic is under the car.

*For *children* the singular is *child.*

Practice

C. Ask about the location of each person or thing listed below. Then answer your question.

1. man

Where's the man?
He's at the office.

2. police officer

3. bird

4. lamp

5. key

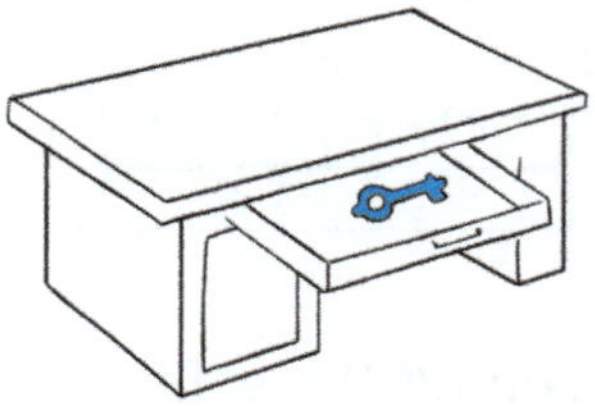

D. Draw the objects and the person in the places named below.

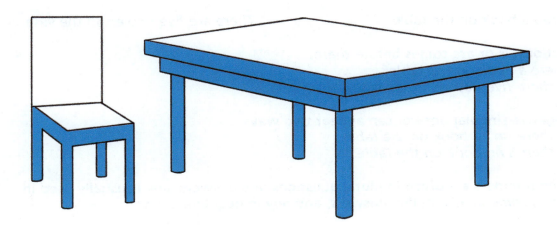

1. a bowl on the table

2. flowers in the bowl

3. a picture above the chair

4. a lamp on the table

5. a pair of boots under the table

6. a book between the bowl and the lamp

7. a cat behind the chair

8. a person in the chair

VOCABULARY

above	boy	front (in front of)	little	sofa
at	car	girl	office	suitcase
behind	child	home	on	under
between	children	in	park	wall
big	door	key	picture	where
book	drawer	lamp	seat	where's
bowl				

THERE IS, THERE ARE; SOME, ANY

There + *is* or *are* shows that something exists in a particular place. *There is (there's)* is used with singular nouns. *There are* is used with plural nouns.

There's a book on the table.

There are five flowers in the vase.

In questions, *is* or *are* comes before *there*.
Is there a book on the table?
Are there five flowers in the vase?

The negative singular answer can appear two ways.
No, there isn't a book on the table.
No, there's no book on the table.

When no numbers are given in plural questions and answers, *any* is usually used in questions, *some* in affirmative answers, and *any* in negative answers.

Are there any flowers in the vase?
No, there aren't any flowers in the vase.

Are there any plants on the floor?
Yes, there are some plants on the floor.

There's a table in the dining room.

There are four plates on the table.

There are some napkins on the table.

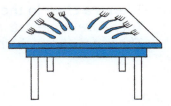

There are some forks on the table.

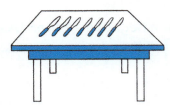

There are some knives* on the table.

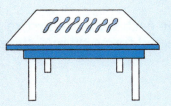

There are some spoons on the table.

There are two bananas on the table.

There are three bowls of vegetables on the table.

There's a salt shaker on the table.

There's a pepper shaker on the table.

*The singular of *knives* is *knife*.

Practice

A. Substitute the words in this sentence.

> **EXAMPLE:** There's *a chair* in the room. (some cats/three chairs)
> *There are some cats in the room.*
> *There are three chairs in the room.*

1. a TV

2. two tables

3. three pictures

4. a window

5. some lamps

6. a sofa

7. some bowls

8. a bird

9. two dogs

10. a fish

11. a computer

12. a book

B. Change each sentence first to a question and then to a negative answer. Use the contracted forms *there's, there's no,* and *there aren't any*.

1. There's a salt shaker on the table.
   Is there a salt shaker on the the table?
   No, there's no salt shaker on the table.

2. There are some chairs in the kitchen.
   Are there any chairs in the kitchen?
   No, there aren't any chairs in the kitchen.

3. There are some boys and girls in the park.

4. There are some plates on the table.

5. There are some vegetables in the bowl.

6. There's a fork on the plate.

7. There are some napkins on the table.

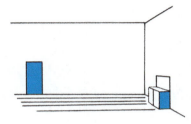

8. There are some pictures on the wall.

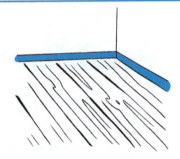

9. There are some plants on the floor.

10. There are some flowers in the vase.

11. There's a shirt in the suitcase.

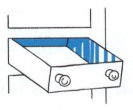

12. There are some keys in the drawer.

Practice

C. **Answer the questions in complete sentences. Use contractions when possible.**

1. Is there a spoon or a fork on this plate?
There's a fork on this plate.

2. Are there flowers or bananas in this bowl?

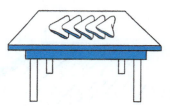

3. Are there plates or napkins on this table?

4. Is there a vase or a pepper shaker on this table?

VOCABULARY	any	five	fork	kitchen	napkin
	dining room	floor	four	knife	pepper shaker

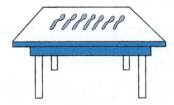

5. Are there napkins or spoons on this table?

6. Is there a table or a chair in this kitchen?

7. Are there cats or dogs under this table?

8. Is there a plant or a lamp on this desk?

plant	salt shaker	spoon	three	vase
plate	some	there	two	vegetable

POSSESSIVE ADJECTIVES; POSSESSIVE PRONOUNS

8

The possessive adjective comes before the noun it modifies and agrees in gender and number with the possessor, not the noun.

I have my key.   *I have their key.*
I have my keys.   *I have their keys.*

Use a possessive pronoun to avoid repeating the noun.

This key is my key.   *This key is mine.*
These keys are my keys.   *These keys are mine.*

SINGULAR			PLURAL		
Subject	Possessive Adjective	Possessive Pronoun	Subject	Possessive Adjective	Possessive Pronoun
I	my	mine	we	our	ours
you	your	yours	you	your	yours
he	his	his			
she	her	hers	they	their	theirs
it	its	its			

It's my raincoat.
It's your raincoat.

Mine is long.
Yours is short.

It's his suitcase.

His is big.

5

It's her suitcase.

6

Hers is little.

7

Where are our hats?

8

They are ours.

9

Where are your CDs?

10

They are yours.

11

It's their barbecue.

12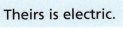

Theirs is electric.

Practice

A. Substitute the words in italics in the sentences with a new possessive adjective and a corresponding possessive pronoun.

> EXAMPLE: They are *our* hats. They are *ours*. (your)
> *They are your hats. They are yours.*

1. my   **2.** his   **3.** their   **4.** her

B. Answer the questions. First give an affirmative answer and then a negative answer.

1. Is it her CD or yours?
> *It's her CD.*
> *It isn't mine.*

2. Is it your hat or his?

3. Are they their raincoats or ours?

4. Is it my sandwich or yours?

5. Are they our books or yours?

6. Are they his boots or hers?

7. Is it his milkshake or hers?

Practice

8. Is it her key or mine?

9. Are they your bicycles or theirs?

10. Is it her dish or ours?

11. Are they their socks or ours?

12. Is it our barbecue or theirs?

C. Rewrite the sentences using the verb *to be* and the correct possessive pronoun.

1. I own the house.
The house is mine.

2. John owns the bicycles.

3. Patricia owns the short dress.

4. We own the lamps.

5. Mr. Smith owns the long raincoat.

6. The woman owns the big hat.

7. Ana and Jeff own the plants.

8. The boy owns the shoes.

9. You own the barbecue.

10. I own the big bowl.

VOCABULARY

barbecue	hat	long	ours	their
bicycle	her	milkshake	own	theirs
CD	hers	mine	raincoat	your
dish	his	my	sandwich	yours
electric	its	our	short	

THE INDEFINITE ARTICLE: *A or An*

Use *a* or *an* with singular nouns that can be counted:

a pear   pears   an apple   apples

Use *a* before a consonant sound: *a pen, a book.*
Use *an* before a vowel sound: *an apple, an orange.*

1

This is an office.

2

This is an envelope.

3
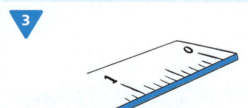
This is an inch.

4

This is an airplane.

Note: Use the definite article *the* with specific or particular nouns, either singular or plural.

5

This is an umbrella.

6

This is an earring.

7

This is an orange.

8

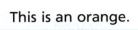

This is an egg.

9

This is an arm.

10

This is an eye.

11

This is an ear.

12

This is an elephant.

Practice

A. **Fill in the blanks with _a_ or _an_.**

1. This is ___an___ airplane.

2. This is ___a___ radio.

3. This is _____ earring.

4. This is _____ orange.

5. This is _____ pear.

6. This is _____ elephant.

7. This is _____ ear.

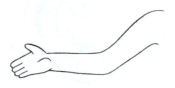

8. This is _____ arm.

9. This is _____ egg.

10. This is _____ television.*

11. This is _____ desk.

12. This is _____ office.

13. This is _____ envelope.

14. This is _____ umbrella.

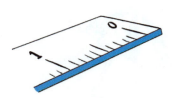

15. This is _____ inch.

16. This is _____ computer.

*A television is often called a *TV*.

Practice

B. Fill in the blanks with *a* or *an* and the name of the object.

1. This is ___*a table*___.

2. This is ___*an earring*___.

3. This is _____.

4. This is _____.

5. This is _____.

6. This is _____.

7. This is _____.

8. This is _____.

9. This is _____.

10. This is _____.

11. This is _____.

12. This is _____.

C. Substitute the words in this sentence.

EXAMPLE: This is a *book.*   (eye/ house)
This is an eye.
This is a house.

1. chair

2. arm

3. ear

4. orange

5. earring

6. TV

7. egg

8. envelope

9. inch

10. office

11. school

12. apple

13. shoe

14. elephant

15. radio

16. umbrella

VOCABULARY	airplane	arm	egg	inch	television
	an	ear	envelope	orange	umbrella
	apple	earring	eye	pear	

PLURAL OF NOUNS

Form the plural of nouns in the following ways:

1. Add *-s* to most nouns.

| one book | two books | one calculator | two calculators |

2. Add *-es* to most nouns that end in *-s, -sh, -ch,* or *-x*. Pronounce *-es* as a separate syllable.

| one box | two boxes | one bus | two buses |

3. Some nouns end in a consonant followed by *-y*. They usually form the plural by dropping the *-y* and adding *-ies*.

| one fly | two flies | one dictionary | two dictionaries |

4. Some nouns have special plural forms.

| one tooth | two teeth | one foot | two feet |

| one man | two men | one woman | two women |

| one child | two children | one person | two people |

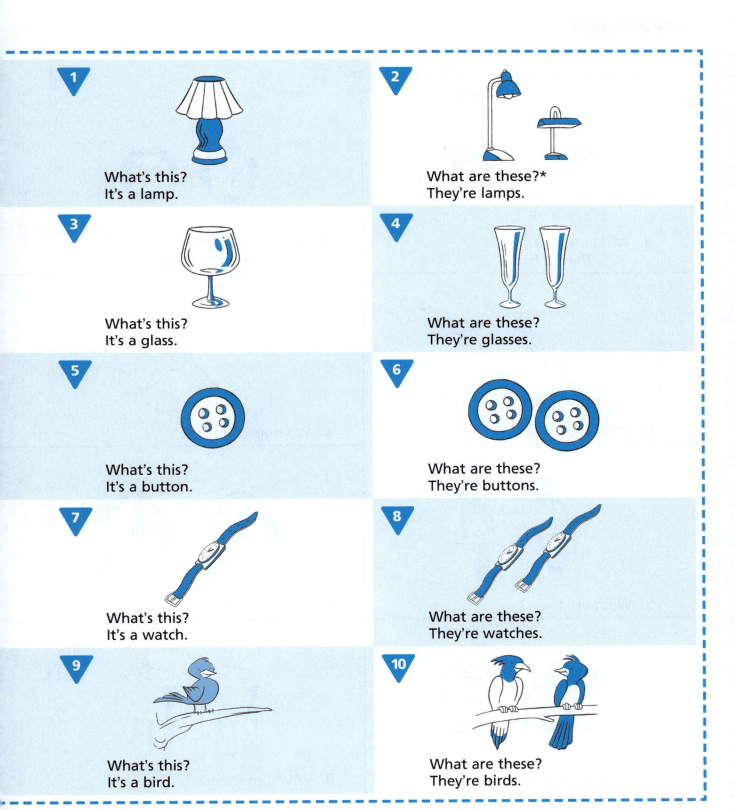

1 What's this?
It's a lamp.

2 What are these?*
They're lamps.

3 What's this?
It's a glass.

4 What are these?
They're glasses.

5 What's this?
It's a button.

6 What are these?
They're buttons.

7 What's this?
It's a watch.

8 What are these?
They're watches.

9 What's this?
It's a bird.

10 What are these?
They're birds.

*The plural of *this* is *these*. *They're* is the contraction of *they are*.

Practice

A. Answer the questions in complete sentences.

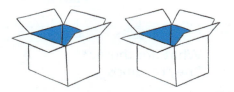

1. What are these?
They're boxes.

2. What are these?
They're buttons.

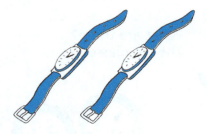

3. What are these?

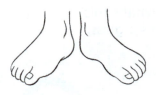

4. What are these?

5. What are these?

6. What are these?

7. What are these?

8. What are these?

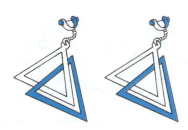

9. What are these?

10. What are these?

11. What are these?

12. What are these?

13. What are these?

14. What are these?

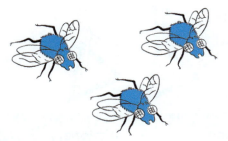

15. What are these?

16. What are these?

Practice

B. Fill in the blanks with the correct plural form.

1. They're _____*envelopes*_____.

2. They're _____.

3. They're _____.

4. They're _____.

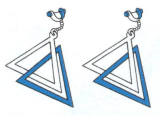

5. They're _____.

VOCABULARY	box	bus	button	dictionary	fly

6. They're _____.

7. They're _____.

8. They're _____.

9. They're _____.

10. They're _____.

| foot | glass | one | these | tooth | watch |

DEMONSTRATIVE PRONOUNS:
Singular and Plural

This (singular) and *these* (plural) point out something near.
That (singular) and *those* (plural) point out something at a distance.
That's is the contraction of *that is*.

This is a door.
That's a window.

This is a refrigerator.
That's a stove.

This is a car.
That's a boat.

This is a stamp.
That's an envelope.

This is a letter.
That's a mailbox.

These are doors.
Those are windows.

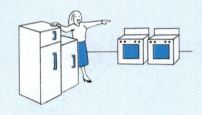

These are refrigerators.
Those are stoves.

These are cars.
Those are boats.

These are stamps.
Those are envelopes.

These are letters.
Those are mailboxes.

Practice

1. This is a horse.
These are horses.

3. That's a letter.

5. This is a boat.

7. That's an envelope.

2. That's a chalkboard.
Those are chalkboards.

4. This is a stamp.

6. That's a refrigerator.

8. That's a watch.

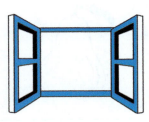

9. This is a window.

10. That's a fly.

11. This is a door.

12. That's a car.

13. That's an umbrella.

14. This is a child.

15. This is a mailbox.

16. That's an island.

Practice

B. Fill in the blanks using *Is this* or *Are these* to complete the questions. Then answer the questions with *It's* or *They're*.

1. _____*Is this*_____ an apple or a pear?

_____*It's a pear*_____ .

2. _____ a desk or a chalkboard?

_____ .

3. _____ dogs or horses?

_____ .

4. _____ a boat or a car?

_____ .

5. _____ dresses or coats?

_____ .

VOCABULARY	boat	island	letter	mailbox	refrigerator

C. Fill in the blanks using *Is that* or *Are those* to complete the questions. Then answer the questions with *It's* or *They're.*

1. _____*Is that*_____ a skirt or a pair of pants?

_____*It's a skirt*_____.

2. _____ calculators or computers?

_____.

3. _____ an elephant or a horse?

_____.

4. _____ a bird or an airplane?

_____.

5. _____ cars or buses?

_____.

| stamp | stove | that | that's | those |

NUMBERS:
Cardinals and Ordinals

12

These numbers are used for counting. They answer the question "How many?"

CARDINAL NUMBERS

0	zero	**10**	ten	**20**	twenty
1	one	**11**	eleven	**21**	twenty-one
2	two	**12**	twelve	**22**	twenty-two
3	three	**13**	thirteen	**23**	twenty-three
4	four	**14**	fourteen	**24**	twenty-four
5	five	**15**	fifteen	**25**	twenty-five
6	six	**16**	sixteen	**26**	twenty-six
7	seven	**17**	seventeen	**27**	twenty-seven
8	eight	**18**	eighteen	**28**	twenty-eight
9	nine	**19**	nineteen	**29**	twenty-nine

30	thirty	**101**	one hundred one
31	thirty-one	**102**	one hundred two
40	forty	**200**	two hundred
41	forty-one	**201**	two hundred one
50	fifty	**300**	three hundred
60	sixty	**400**	four hundred
70	seventy	**500**	five hundred
80	eighty	**1,000**	one thousand
90	ninety	**1,001**	one thousand one
100	one hundred	**2,000**	two thousand

Addition

Two plus three { is / equals } five. $2 + 3 = 5$

Five plus six is eleven. $5 + 6 = 11$

Subtraction

Seven minus four is three. $7 - 4 = 3$

Nine minus five is four. $9 - 5 = 4$

Multiplication

Two times eight is sixteen. $2 \times 8 = 16$

Four times seven is twenty-eight. $4 \times 7 = 28$

Division

Eight divided by four is two. $8 \div 4 = 2$

Twenty divided by two is ten. $20 \div 2 = 10$

ORDINAL NUMBERS

These are numbers like *first, second, third, fourth, fifth, sixth, seventh, eighth, ninth, tenth, eleventh, twelfth*. They describe position or order in a series.

This is my *first* English class. I live on the *twelfth* floor.

Practice

A. Fill in the blanks with the correct number word. Read the sentences aloud.

1. There are _____*three*_____ dogs.

2. There are _____ earrings.

3. There are _____ movie stars.

4. There are _____ bananas.

5. There are _____ bananas.

6. There are _____ cars.

7. There are _____ floors.

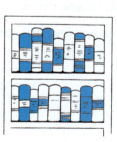

8. There are _____ books.

B. Complete each sentence with the correct ordinal number.

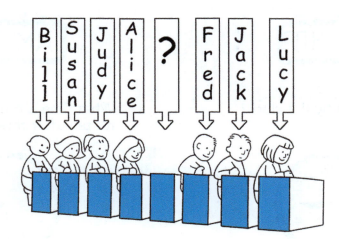

1. Lucy is in the _____*first*_____ seat.

2. Bill is in the _____ seat.

3. Fred is in the _____ seat.

4. Alice is in the _____ seat.

5. Jack is in the _____ seat.

6. Susan is in the _____ seat.

7. Nobody is in the _____ seat.

8. Judy is in the _____ seat.

TELLING TIME; COUNTING MONEY

What time is it by this clock?
It's four o'clock.

What time is it now?
It's ten after three.

What time is it now?
It's a quarter after three.   OR
It's three fifteen.

What time is now?
It's half past three.   OR
It's three thirty.

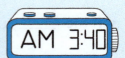

What time is it now?
It's twenty to four.   OR
It's three forty.

What time is it now?
It's a quarter to four.   OR
It's three forty-five.

What time is it?
It's 7 A.M.*

What time is it?
It's 10 P.M.**

*A.M. indicates the morning hours from midnight to noon.
**P.M. indicates the afternoon and evening hours from noon to midnight.

Dollars are usually made of paper.

Cents are metal coins.

A penny is worth one cent.*

A nickel is worth five cents.

A dime is worth ten cents.

A quarter is worth twenty-five cents.

A half-dollar is worth fifty cents.

There is also a dollar coin.

*A dollar is worth one hundred pennies.

Practice

A. What time is it?

1.

2.

3.

4.

5.

6.

7.

8.

9.

10.

11.

12.